The Man Talk
A 'Rites of Passage'
Advice From A Father
To His Son
"Boyhood to Manhood"

101 Life Lessons Every Young Man <u>Needs</u> To Learn
By Michael Abasi Olefemi
(selected poems by Carolyn Dennis-Roundtree)

ISBN 10 1500911356
ISBN 13 9781500911355
Copyright ©2004
Printed by Free Minds Free Spirit

Table of Contents

Part I 'Drama for Drama'

James And Jesus 'Dangerous Minds'	pg. 10
It's Drama For Drama	pg. 12
Keep It Real	pg. 13
Your 'Rep'	pg. 14
Don't Let Yo' Mouth Write A Check Yo' Ass can't Cash	pg. 15
To Get Out Of 'Da Hood'	pg. 16
If You Are Friends With A Fool	pg. 17
You Gotta' Have Heart	pg. 18
Mine Yo' Own	pg. 19
Standing On NO!	pg. 20
You Pay What You Owe	pg. 21
My Last Day	pg. 22
Respect The Police	pg. 27
God Is Real	pg. 29
All Money Ain't Good Money	pg. 30
Punked Once, Punked For Life	pg. 31
Put Up Or Shut Up!	pg. 32
Style Is Everything	pg. 33
Playing 'Da Dozens'	pg. 34
Your Friends Will Make You Or Break You	pg. 35
If You Can't Stand On Your Own	pg. 36
Blood Is Thicker Than Water	pg. 37

Signatures	pg. 38
Everything Has Value	pg. 41
Men/Boys Who Hit Girls Show Their Weakness	pg. 42
Fighting With Your Hands	pg. 43
Education Is To Be Respected	pg. 44
Watch Yo' Back	pg. 45
Young Girls Use Sex	pg. 46
Young Boys Use Their Size	pg. 47
CD (Carlos Diaz)	pg. 48
From Rags To Riches	pg. 52
Everybody's Got A Hustle	pg. 53
'Playa Playa'	pg. 54
Nothing Comes Easy	pg. 59
Don't Be Afraid To Get Dirty	pg. 60
Guys Will Trip On You About Their Girl	pg. 61
The Old School Rule	pg. 63
Nobody Makes It Out On Their Own	pg. 64
'Save The Drama'	pg. 65
Don't Start None, Won't Be None	pg. 66
'Willie Lump Lump'	pg. 67
Word Is Bond	pg. 68
Stay Out of it'	pg. 69
Blind Leading The Blind	pg. 70
Don't Date Your Friend's Sister	pg. 71
The Color Of Your Skin	pg. 72
Grand People	pg. 74

Part II "On the Real"

Bullets Have No Name	pg. 78
'Niggaz'	pg. 79
You Could Die Over A Dime	pg. 80
Gangs Are Dysfunctional	pg. 81
Your Manhood, Your Money, Your Woman	pg. 82
In 'Da Hood', People Die All The Time	pg. 83
'Caught Up In The Game'	pg. 84
Any Coward Can Pull A Trigger	pg. 85
In 'Da Hood', The Innocent Gets Hurt Too	pg. 86
Every Man For Himself	pg. 87
If You Gotta Run To Get A Gun	pg. 88
Violence Isn't The Way	pg. 89
Every Ma for Himself	pg. 90
By Any Means Necessary	pg. 91
The Killing Fields	pg. 92
You Gotta Bring Some, To Get Some	pg. 93
Everybody Don't Make It Out	pg. 94
Take Threats Seriously	pg. 95
Sometimes You Get, Sometimes You Give	pg. 96
The Big Question About Sex	pg. 97

Stronger Than The Streets — pg. 98

Part III "Back in the Day"

Affirmations — pg. 106
Grandma' and Grandpa' — pg. 108
A Praying Mother — pg. 109
The House Is To Be Protected — pg. 110
Back In The Day — pg. 111
Children Were Seen, Not Heard — pg. 112
Spirits Waiting — pg. 113
Hoop Dreams — pg. 116
Umoja — pg. 121
Home Grown Variety — pg. 124
The End Of The Matter — pg. 127

Research Based Rites of Passage Program

Introduction

Arnold Van Gennep's 1996 publication of "les rites de passage" used the phrase rites of passage. Mensah (1991) defined rites of passage as: Those **structures, rituals, and ceremonies** by which age-class members or individuals in a group **successfully come to know who they are and what they are about**, the purpose and meaning for their existence, as they **proceed from one clearly defined state of existence to the next state** of passage in their lives. (p.62)

Rites of Passage in Higher Education

Tinto's (1988) model of student departure (graduation) is based on Van Gennep's work on the rites of passage. Tinto stated: We begin our development of a theory of student departure by turning to the field of social anthropology and studies of the process of establishing membership in traditional societies. Specifically, we turn to the work of Arnold Van Gennep and his study of the rites of passage in tribal societies. …He saw life as being comprised of a series of passages leading individuals from birth to death and from membership in one group or status to another. (p.91)

'Rites of Passage' Workshop- STARS
(**S**tudents **A**chieving and **R**eaching **S**uccess)

The Kupita/Transiciones Model was created to support the academic and social needs of participants. The guiding principles of the **Nguzo Saba (Seven Principles of Kwanzaa)** were used to ensure a holistic approach to the student's needs. These principles are 1). **Purpose** 2). **Unity** 3). **Self-determination** 4). **Creativity** 5). **Cooperation** 6). **Collective Responsibility** 7). **Faith.** The Man Talk 'Rites of Passage' Program integrates all seven of these elements within its 'Boyhood to Manhood' modules. Seven interactive workshops which emphasizes these concepts are developed to challenge the participants to engage in growth activities that demonstrate their acquisition of the Rites of Passage concepts which will lead them from 'Boyhood to Manhood'. After successful completion of each module participants participate in a cultural ceremony which recognizes and shows appreciation for their accomplishment in front of family, friends and their community. The typical 'Rites of Passage' program is from one to three days, four hours per day. For more information on how to develop and implement this program please contact Michael Dennis at 310-613-3316 or via email at michaeldennism@aol.com.

Part 1

"Drama for Drama"

"James and Jesus"

By Carolyn Dennis-Roundtree

Me and my homie Jesus are 15...
We are endangered and dangerous...
so they say.
Uneducated. Unemployed. Undisciplined.
Born with "three strikes."
Black/brown, poor, and male
We are hot...too hot.
Filled with longing
for more than what we got
and anger at those who
stand in our way.
Me and my homie Jesus are 15...
and have low self-esteem.
We are almost sure
to be statistics.
To be jailed, drugged or killed
before we are 25...
 so we think.
We think,
believe, everything is cool.
We lean in the wind
Smiling that sad smile,
Playing that costly game...
In ignorance.

My son, your journey begins...

My son...

"It's drama for drama"

Each situation you find yourself in will give you back an equal response to your response to it (you reap what you sew). Whatever you do to others, the same will be done to you. If you give good and honesty, you will receive good and honesty back. If you do bad and dishonest things to others, bad and dishonest things will be done to you. Don't be the one who brings the drama...then drama won't come your way. Now if someone steps to you with drama, let them know you're not down with that drama. If they don't stop, then you will have to let them know that you're willing to return 'drama for drama'. But only do this when they give you no other choice.

My son...

"Keep it real"

Whatever you do, don't be a fake. Nobody wants to be around a fake person. When you're fake, people don't know where you stand because you keep changing. When people don't know where you stand, they don't trust you. If they don't trust you, they won't look out for you. Also, if you're a fake, you won't attract the kind of friends who you can trust because they're probably fake too. Be yourself. Don't change just to get people to like you. People either will like you or they won't. Either way it goes, being fake ain't cool. "If you don't stand for something, you'll fall for anything." Fake people don't stand for anything.

My son...

"Your reputation is developed
by what you <u>don't</u> do"

It's easy to "go along with the crowd", but it requires strength not to be a follower. You're going to have to 'dig deep' to not join a gang or any group that does things that could get you in trouble. Dig deep, it's there you will find your true strength...
and others will follow you. You get more respect by what you say no to, then what you say yes to. People expect you to be a follower (that's what most people your age are). But if you really want to get respect, be the kind of person that makes his own choices (you might even have to fight, like I had to, because there's going to be someone who's going to try to <u>make</u> you be down with them). Never let anyone dictate to you what and who you should be down with.

Get with me at <u>michaeldennism@aol.com</u>

My son…

"Don't let your mouth write a check
  your ass can't cash"

Watch what you say and who you say it to. Don't be out there bragging about what you can do, what you're gonna do, and who you're gonna do it to. Nobody likes a 'big mouth'. As a matter of fact when you're a big mouth, you make yourself a target. There's always somebody out there that wants to be the one who shuts up the 'big mouth'. Every 'big mouth' that I've ever known has said the wrong thing, at the wrong time, to the wrong person, and got their asses kicked for it. Don't bring this kind of negative attention to yourself. Better yet, just chill. Nobody likes a 'big mouth, but everybody likes the 'cool' quiet guy.

My son...

"To get out of 'da hood',
you gotta really want to!

You gotta see yourself beyond 'da hood'. Beyond the gangs, the drugs, the violence (don't be naïve and try to act like they don't exist, that's when you get caught slippin', but don't let these things be your main focus). You gotta expect more for yourself than the negative things you see, and hear, and live in. You gotta have an 'I refuse to settle for less' attitude, a 'whatever it takes mentality'. You gotta first decide what you want, next find out what you have to do to get it, and then go for it. Keep looking forward, and don't look back. That's how you get out. That's how I got out. Oh, you can ask me for advice anytime 'cause I got yo' back.

My son...

> "If you're friends with a fool, you the fool"

I once had a fool for a friend because I felt sorry for him. But after he crashed my car and pulled a gun on me because I asked him to pay for the damages, and then laughed in my face telling me, "You the fool for letting me do what I did. You knew I was a fool." To say the least, he was no longer my friend (I felt like hurting this dude). But I realized he was right. If you put your life into the hands of a fool (a person who does stupid things without thinking about the negative consequences), then you can expect to suffer from some of those negative consequences. Don't try to teach a fool notto be a fool. They'll laugh at you. That's who they are. Just get away from them. Save yourself. Let that fool learn from the school of hard knocks.

My son...

"You gotta have heart"

I won't lie to you, you can't be no punk. You're gonna be tested. So prepare for battle. Don't be afraid. Them dudes out there can smell fear. If they think you're scared, then they're gonna keep steppin' to you, keep testing you. We use to say, "If you're scared, stay at home" (but sooner or later you're gonna have to come out for something). Fear will take your heart, steal your dreams, crush your hopes. You gotta have heart to conquer your fear. Don't be afraid of them dudes out there, they ain't nobody. They ain't tough. If you saw any of them by themselves they would be afraid of you. They only act tough when they got back up. Don't ever let anybody 'take yo' heart'. Without it, you can never be a man. Trust me on this.

My son...

"Mine yo' own is a bunch of bullshit!"

See no evil, hear no evil, speak no evil is the reason why our 'hoods are in the terrible conditions they're in. You gotta do what's right in your heart. You don't have to 'snitch', but you can get involved in helping things to get better. You can talk to some of your homies about chillin' out on some of that dumb stuff they do. You can help our neighbor (especially the single mothers) by looking out for their children. You can help by volunteering to keep the 'hood clean. Most of all, don't you trip. Let me tell you, those dudes out there talkin' 'bout, 'Snitches get stitches' are the first ones to 'drop a dime' when the judge gets ready to drop some time on that ass. Trust me on this.

My son...

"Standing on NO!
Is the first lesson of manhood"

This is the beginning of wisdom, of character, of strength. Let no mean no! Don't waiver. Think about what you're being asked, and then speak. Being able to say no, and really mean it, will save your life. A lot of people can say no once or twice, but then they give in. Even if you have to say no a thousand times that's o.k. Never say yes when you really mean no. But this isn't easy to do because there are a lot of things out there you will want to try, but shouldn't. Saying no isn't easy, but it's necessary. No has to come from the heart. You can even be cool about it. When someone asks you to do something you don't want to, just say, "Man, I'm cool on that". Every man needs to have a standard. Knowing what you will or won't do, that's your standard.

My son...

> "You pay what you owe;
> one way or another"

There's no way around this. There's no easy way out. When it comes to this, no one can or will save you. Not even me. You either pay as required, or they will take it out yo' ass. This is serious, especially when it comes to owing somebody money. I won't lie to you, if you don't pay them, then they're gonna try to hurt you (especially those dudes in 'da hood'). That's just the way it is. Nobody breaks this rule and gets away with it. It divides families, turns friends into enemies, and stokes the flames of 'pay back' (getting even, by whatever it takes). Either way, 'Man up'. Pay what you owe. Better yet 'owe no man'. If you can't afford it, do without it.

MY LAST DAY "THE DRIVE BY"

I was just standing there,
that's all.
I didn't even know what was happening.
Just rapping with my friends.
Sipping a little gin.
I had no idea this would be my end.

I was just 'a laughing.
With a big bright smile on my face.
With my big crooked teeth, my deep black eyes.
Oh God, it seems such a waste.

I was just standing there,
that's all.
Talking about my new girl friend.
And that I was starting school again.
And did the Raiders win?

I was just 'a smiling, I can still hear my voice.
I coughed, "Those cigarettes", I thought.
And I sounded kind of hoarse.
Oh God, couldn't you have made
me change my course?

You see my moms raised me right.
Took me to church Sunday morning and night.

I had good "role models" in my life.
It was me who chose wrong over right.
I was just standing there,
that's all.
Although my moms told me to come home.
And to leave those streets alone.
But I thought that I was grown.
Although in my heart I knew that I was wrong.

I was just standing there,
that's all.
Just finished playing some basketball.

When the cars swung around.
And I shouted," What ya' claiming clown?!"
And we all hit the ground.

Then the bullets came screaming.
Like a dragon's breath- fire breathing.
Like being in a nightmare, while daydreaming.
Next you're holding me in your arms,
my blood hot, steaming.
But inside I'm cold, freezing.
And I'm still not believing.

That the bullets shot me down.
Then there was no sound....
But me dying...
and you crying.

And my last thought was...
I should have paid 'dem dudes their money

Rites Of Passage-Rewards-Applying Wisdom

"Being obedient to wise advice can put you in the right place at the right time." "Being disobedient does the opposite, it puts you in the wrong place at the wrong time."

Do you agree or disagree with this quote? Explain why or why not.

How will you personally apply wisdom in your life to avoid similar situations?

My son...

"Respect the police"

I know you've heard "F- - - - the police", but I tell you, "Respect the police". Most police who work in 'da hood' are honest, caring, hard working men and women. They have saved more lives and volunteered more of their time than almost anybody else. The police are just like you, regular people. A lot of them come from the same neighborhoods we come from. Some of my closest friends are police. Police are some of the 'down-est, coolest' people I know. So check that drama about not liking the police. The people who hate the police the most are the ones who are doing things they shouldn't be doing. Treat them with respect and they will show that respect back to you. Respect is a two way street. You gets none, unless you give some'. When you're dealing with the police always begin by saying, "Yes sir." These two little words will take you a long way. These two little words will get you back home alive. Trust me.

My son…

"God is real, and he's always with you."

God is not a 'thing' way out there (in the heavens). God is a person, not a thing. God is closer to you than anything or anybody. God is in your heart. God is hope when you lose your way. God is love. God loves you more than any person could ever love you. God will never leave you. God will always see you through. God will never fail you. To find God all you have to do is call Him. Just say "Lord Jesus", and he will answer. I promise you. I'm living proof.

My Son...

'All money ain't good money'

Some money is 'blood money' (money gotten from doing something illegal or immoral). This kind of money comes with a price. If its drug money, that means someone is being hurt either by doing the drugs, selling the drugs or stealing to get the drugs. If it's money gotten by theft that means something was taken from somebody who is innocent. If it's money gotten through violence, then someone was hurt in order to get the money (which means they will be seeking revenge). If its money gotten through sexual means i.e. pimping, prostitution etc., then that's a moral issue (something they will regret as they get older). Never go against your morals, your values. Any money you get by others being hurt 'ain't good money' its 'blood money'.

Get with me at michaeldennism@aol.com

My son...

"Punked once, punked for life"

It's better to stand up and get beat down, stand up and get beat down, stand up and get beat down, than to never stand up at all. It doesn't matter if you win or lose, it only matters that you keep standing up. Trust me on this. Soon, whoever is messing with you will realize 'you ain't no punk', and that they have a battle on their hands. Eventually, they will back up off you. You don't get respect by backing down, you get respect by standing up. Make no mistake, respect must be 'earned'. It won't be given freely, and you can't buy it. Respect earned is like an eternal flame that burns brightest when it's challenged. You earn your respect by standing your ground.

My son...

"It's put up or shut up"

Remember this, 'those who talk the most probably can't bust a grape'. The more they talk, the smaller they get. A man's actions will speak for him. Be a man of few words, but a lot of action. I've seen so many dudes out there running their mouths talking about what they gonna do, but can't do anything. My son, stay away from them dudes. Where I come from it's 'put up or shut up'. Guys who do, don't talk about it, they're too busy taking care of business. They don't have time to listen to that drama. My son, "Don't talk about it, be about it." "If you gonna talk the talk, you gotta walk the walk." Don't be no punk about what you say. Say what you mean, and do what you say. Or keep yo' damn mouth closed.

Get with me at michaeldennism@aol.com

My son...

> "Style is everything"

You gotta be cool in whatever you do. Whatever you do...do with style, with class, with dignity and with passion. In 'da hood', image and presentation is everything. What's cool about it is that when you are grown this will take you a long way. People like to be around a person that has style and class. I'm not talking about being superficial. I'm talking about how you carry yourself. Carry yourself like you know what you're doing, like you know who you are, like you have confidence in yourself. People dig that. Do your best. Look your best. Dress masculine. Look like a man not a girl. Be the best you at all times. You only get one chance to make a first impression. This is how you set yourself apart from the rest.

Get with me at michaeldennism@aol.com

My son...

"'Playing the dozens' can get you hurt, or worse, killed"

You can break a man using words and it's just as real as breaking him using a baseball bat. If, by your words (or actions), you take a man's dignity, he will strike back at you in the worse way he can, the worse way possible. He has nothing else to lose and everything to gain. Playing the dozens isn't a 'kid's game'. Remember my son, some people just 'don't play that'. So don't you play that either. I never played the dozens because I knew if you said something about my moms, then I was gonna handle you. So since I didn't play them, others respected that, and didn't play them on me. Besides, I didn't think it was funny to talk about somebody moms. They can say whatever about you, but tell them to leave moms out of it. That's real talk.

Get with me at michaeldennism@aol.com

My son...

"Your friends will 'make or break' you"

If you want true friends, then you must be a true friend. You attract what you are. Choose your friends wisely, because yo' enemies will choose you, whether you want them to or not. Sometimes it's more important to know who got yo' back than who's back stabbing. Your true friends will protect you from the 'back stabbers'.
My son, if you're lucky you're going to have two or three true friends in your life. These guys (or girls) will be down for you for life. You can trust your life to them. But this kind of friendship is earned not just by your words, but by your deeds as well. It will take years for your friendship to get to this level, but it will. What they do for you, you will have to do the same for them.

Get with me at michaeldennism@aol.com

My son...

"If you can't stand on your own,
then you can't stand with others"

It is impossible to be a help to others when you can't help yourself. You can't add strength to others when you don't have any. Don't be the kind of man that needs others before you can make a stand. A real man has to be able to stand alone, and then others will follow. There will be things that nobody can do for you. Nobody's going to give you a good education; you're going to have to get it yourself. Nobody's going to give you a good job; you're going to have to get it yourself. When you're grown, nobody's going to raise your children for you; you have to raise them yourself. If you do wrong, nobody's going to do time for you, you have to do it yourself. A real man must be able to stand alone before he can stand with others. Trust me on this.

Get with me at michaeldennism@aol.com

My son....

"Blood is always thicker than water"

You never turn your back on your family, no matter what. If they do wrong, you tell them they're doing wrong and help them through it. If they keep doing wrong, you don't help them to keep doing wrong, but be there for them when they're ready to change. Family is all you got. Your friends will never be there for you like family will. You can choose your friends but you can't choose your family. Don't let anybody make you turn on your family. Yeah, you're going to have ups and downs with your family, but when everybody else fails you, they'll be there. Even if you turn on them, they'll be there to take you back. No friend is gonna' do that for you. Trust me on this.

SIGNATURES
(firmas)
By Carolyn Dennis-Roundtree

You clothe yourself
in signatures...
Cardin, Vuitton, Gucci, Tommy,
Sean John.
Hide from the realness
of sharing.
Forget the purposeful, respectful simple ways
your ancestors lived
"Down South",
"South of the Boarder",

You're cool, too cool.
Smooth, too smooth.
Smart, too smart.
Conceited...
too good for your own good.
This Confused man
whose birthplace is mine too.

You hunt for the "fool's gold" of life.
Saying, "All money is good money"
(*even blood money*).

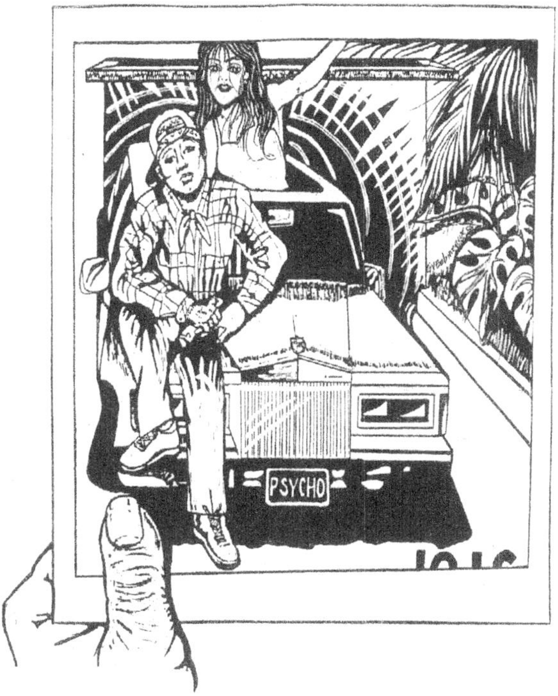
PSYCHO

I say,
You forgot how good
it feels to be happy, nappy,
straight, and curly
in love....being yourself.
(en amor siendo como el es),

Your "real" self,
without the superficial signatures.
This fake man
This sick man
Who is an American
too.

My son...

> "Everything has value,
> even the superficial,
> to those who are shallow"

Designer brand clothes, pimped out cars, a person's looks, how much money they got ...they all count. How much, depends on the person. For you my son, 'things' don't make the man. The man makes the 'things'. When you learn this lesson 'things' can never control you. Superficial people have to have 'things' to feel good about themselves. They put value in the 'things' and not in who they are. The 'things' define them, make or break them. Your real value comes from your heart. How honest you are, how caring you are, how trustworthy you are. No 'thing' can ever be more valuable than that. Trust me on this.

My son...

"Men/boys who hit girls show their weakness, not their strength"

So what, you can beat up a woman/girl. Most men/boys are bigger and stronger than women/girls anyway. You want credit for that?! I don't think so. A guy that does that, I bet he won't step to a dude like that. Punks hit women, not men. If you think your girlfriend is trying to provoke you to hit her (God forbid you are with a girl like that), don't go for it. That's how so many guys end up in jail. Have enough self-control to walk away. That's the only way you can win this fight, by not fighting. Trust me on this.

My son...
"To learn how to fight with your hands is good...to learn how to fight with your head is better"

Knowing how to fight with your hands teaches a young man his boundaries, where he stands with other young men. Hand to hand combat is the measuring stick of a man...but a man is also measured by his intellect. It's good to know that you know how to fight...it's better to know how not to get into a fight. Sometimes the wise move is not to fight, even when you know you can win. When I was growing up I fought not because I wanted to, I had to. That's why I always kept a low profile. It's good to know how to fight if you need to. But if you keep a low profile people won't test you because they don't want to take the chance that you do knowhow to fight. Trust me on this.

Get back with me at
michealdennism@aol.com

My son....

"Education is to be respected, money is to be protected"

Given a choice, choose them both. If you get money (legally of course), continue getting your education. If you get educated, use that knowledge to get money. They both go together because without education you will probably mismanage your money and lose it. And without money, you can't really get a good education. A 'good' education lasts a lifetime and can never be taken away. You can lose all of your money but you can never lose the skills you get from getting a 'good' education. With these skills you can always make more money. I said a 'good' education. Believe me, it's gonna take more than just 'street knowledge' to succeed. If you want to protect your 'paper', get educated. My son, 'a fool and his money are soon departed.' For real.

Get with me at michaeldennism@aol.com

My son...

"Watch yo' back"

Because there's always somebody trying to back stab you. That's life. It is what it is. Besides, it's better to be safe than sorry, or worse, stupid. I once saw a guy pull a gun on my dad, and put the barrel right under his chin. I watched him say something to my dad but I couldn't hear what he was saying. I could see the hate in this man's eyes as he spoke to my dad. My dad got caught slippin' and it could have cost him his life. To this day, I don't know why this guy pulled that gun on my dad (I think it was a robbery). Or why he didn't shoot him. Maybe God put it in his heart that my dad had eight kids at home (at least that's what I want to believe). My advice is, whether you're doing, right or wrong, at church or in the streets, 'watch yo' back'. And whatever you do.

My son…

> "Some young girls are taught to use sex as a weapon"

Whatever has value (real or perceived) has the potential to be used as a weapon. Sex is the master of this game; young girls are its queens. Stay away from this kind of girl. She'll hurt you every way that a girl can hurt a boy (she'll break your heart, she'll take your money, she'll make you do whatever she asks, she'll talk about you behind your back, she'll get with other guys behind your back, she doesn't have any true feelings for you). In 'da hood' we call her 'scanlous' (scandalous). But not all girls are like this. Try to find a girl who wants to get to know you, be friends with you. They use to call these kinds of girls 'good girls'. If you find one, respect her. And always remember, when a girl says no, no means no. Don't play with this.

michaeldennism@aol.com

My son...

"Some young boys are taught to use their size as a weapon to bully others, this is a big mistake"

This is foolish, and could lead to this boy getting seriously hurt. 'Big don't mean bad' and size doesn't mean strength. A boy, no matter what his size, is not a man. A boy can't out think a man. He hasn't lived long enough. When a man looks into the eyes of a boy, he sees this, the doubt in his eyes. I know this because my father gave me that look (I was about fourteen). Respect your elders, respect other men. They didn't get this far for nothing. These are the men who will give you the knowledge you're going to need to survive, to become a man. I don't know it all. My father didn't know it all. But he did know enough to tell me what I'm telling you. Men make men. Trust me on this.

Get with me at michaeldennism@aol.com

CD (Carlos Diaz) A True Story
"The Bigger They Are...
The Harder They Fall"

CD (Carlos Diaz) has been a bully since the time he was born. At the age of 15 he was already 6 feet 5 inches tall and weighed 250 pounds. He never listened to (obeyed) his parents (or anybody else). And wasn't afraid of anybody or anything. It was "whatever, whenever" *(cual sea, cuando sea)*. He was the kind of person who thrived on trouble. CD didn't have to go looking for a gang; the gang was already in him. CD earned his "rep" by beating up people, robbing and stealing, selling drugs, and killing if necessary. CD has *juice; he's a "shot-caller." CD got big 'hood respect. And all who didn't give it to him, he took it. I once saw CD beat a guy up this older guy so bad that he almost killed him. I asked him why he had beat the guy like that, he said, "Why essay? You want some?"

That's how CD was, hard core, stone cold, heartless, unforgiving. I later found out that the guy hadn't done anything to CD. He just did it because he wanted too.

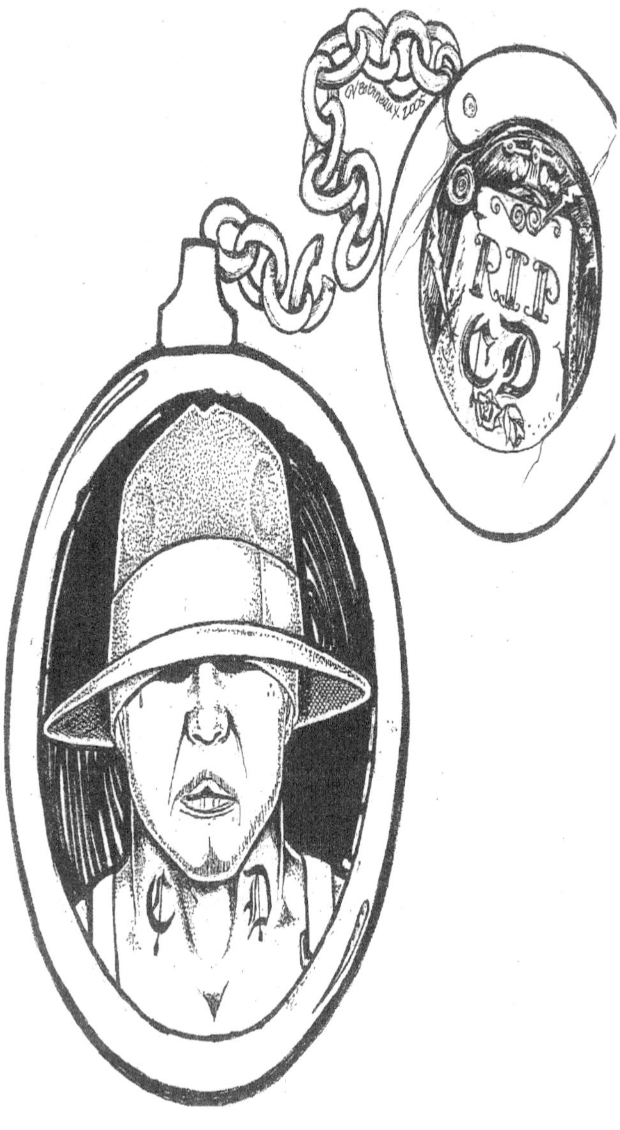
RIP
CD
CD

Two Months Later, CD (Carlos Diaz) thought he was on top of the world. In the 'hood he was "the man", a "King Pin". Everybody gave CD his respect. One night CD was out getting high with the guy he had not long ago almost beaten to death. CD felt safe. He had already punked this guy. "I took his heart. He don't want no more beef with me", CD thought, he was wrong. This same guy pulled out a gun and shot CD to death. CD still has a "rep" but what good is that now? And what's worst, nobody cares." You reap what you sew (you get back what you give)." Charge it to the game.

My son...

Athletics have always been a traditional way to get out of 'da hood' (from 'rags to riches' is every young man's dream). But remember this; always put your education before athletics. Become known as a 'student athlete' not a 'dumb jock'. Go for your dreams. Believe in yourself. But don't let anybody cheat you out of a good education. Get that scholarship. Get that degree and get that professional contract. You can do it all, you can have it all. Trust me on this. I'm living proof.

My Son...

"In 'da hood' everybody's got a hustle"

Everybody's trying to sell you something, make you do something, trying to put you 'up on game'. This is drama, a waste of time. They're only interested in what they can get from you. Steer clear of the hustler, the con man. How do you know if you're being hustled? They always ask you to trust them first. To give them something before they give you something. This is the essence of the 'con game'. Just tell them, "I'm cool" and they won't even try to con you. It's called 'game recognize game'. Trust me.

PLAYA' PLAYA"
    "The Playa' gets Played"
By Michael Dennis

You watched the way I moved through the streets.
You saw the way I smiled.
Wearing brand new clothes
and two hundred dollar shoes
you saw my swagger, I always dressed in style.

I've been sexually active since age thirteen
I learned the "game" from the street *G's.
Using no protection, playing Russian Roulette,
I say, "Me worried about AIDS, homie please?"

You hear the way I talk to one of my girls.
I use that street slang I'm so good at.
You saw the gold tooth shining in my mouth
as I said, "Baby do this, baby do that.
You watch me get in my big "flossy" car.
I tell that young girl,
 "Baby, I'll make you a superstar."
You see me smile and wink, when she says,
"Well let me think?"
As I "dip" on down the boulevard.

You look at me as I speed away.
I say, "Kid stay cool and you'll be
like me some day."

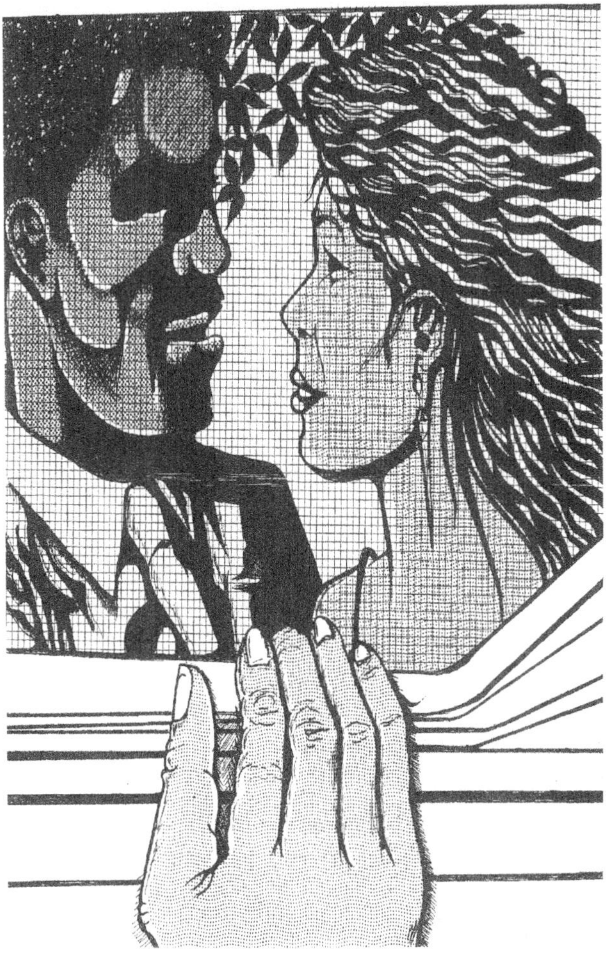

My big bank rolls, my fine platinum chains
my many diamond rings.
My tailor-made suits, my well-groomed hair.
To you I have everything!

You see me hit one of my "girls".
You hear her cry and sob.
And you realized being a PLAYA' is my life
and more than just a job.

You see me snort up some cocaine.
You see me selling dope.
You hear I live way up-town
for you I am your hope.

You watch the police pull me over
for what seemed like no reason at all.
You see them put the handcuffs on me
and say, "Boy, you can have one phone call."

You hear they took away my car.
You hear they kicked me out my house.
They say I'll do hard time now
and it will be three to five before I get out.
You say you'll wait for me until I'm set free.
You want to show me what I did.
I was your role model before you grew up,
yes, when you were just a kid.

But now you're older and you've
"peeped the game."
It's called "All Money Ain't Good Money."
So when they let me out, this time maybe
you can "put me up on the new game", Sonny.

"The New Game" (Sonny's Message)

Well, just last week at the "Playa'z Club"
I saw your girl from back in the days.
I hate to be the one to tell you, Playa'.

She said that she was dying from AIDS.

Now do the math…

The Playa' should have checked himself.
'Cause now the Playa' has gone
and wrecked himself.
Now the Playa' sleeps in the bed he's made.
Now the Playa' is slowly dying from AIDS.

Character Development – Consequences and Repercussions

What were the consequences (punishment) for the PLAYA' mentioned in this poem?

Rites of Passage – Rewards- Applying Obedience

Who is your role model now and why? Explain.

My son...

"In 'da hood', nothing comes easy except drugs and sex"

Drugs kill, sex kills, drugs kill, sex kills, drugs kill, sex kills...get the picture?

My son...

"You can't be afraid to get dirty"

Don't be afraid of hard work, dirty work. That's just the way the world is, hard and gritty, not prissy. So roll up your sleeves, get your hands dirty and get ready to work hard. But I guarantee you; your hard work will pay off. Now go take out he garbage and mow the grass.

My son...

"Some young guys are way
too jealous over their girlfriends"

When you walk by a guy with his girlfriend, don't 'stare her down'. That's being disrespectful. You can give a quick look if you like, but that's all. If she likes you, you'll know and you'll meet her again without him. Trust me. She'll remember how much class you showed and appreciate you for it. It's not weak to show respect. It actually shows the girl how much confidence you have. Besides, how stupid is it to fight over a girl you don't even know? There are some 'fine' girls out there and you're gonna look. If you choose to say something, try this line, "No disrespect to you 'bro, I just wanted to say yo' girl is beautiful." Then keep steppin'. She'll appreciate the compliment, and he'll appreciate the respect. Trust me on this.

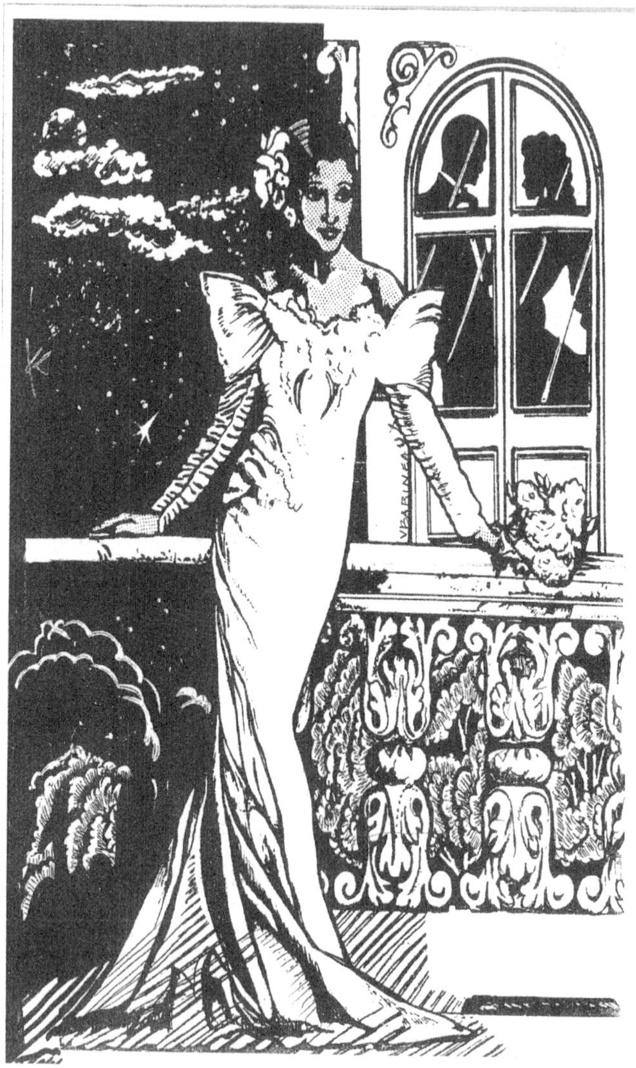

My son…when you grow up,

Remember this 'Old School Rule':
"Always check yo' girl,
 never check the dude."

Do this if you think your girlfriend may be talking to another guy. What I mean by 'check' is to confront her about the situation (no violence). If she wants to be with you, she'll be willing to work it out. If she doesn't, let her go. If you don't want to work it out that's cool too. Don't confront the dude, that will cause violence. Besides, it makes you look like your girlfriend is running you. Like you're so sprung on her that you are jealous of everybody she talks to. Jealousy makes it look like you don't have confidence in yourself. Some girls will use jealousy to control you. Some girls will use jealousy to get you in trouble with other guys. Jealousy is an ugly emotion. Don't be jealous.

Get with me at michaeldennism@aol.com

My son...

"Nobody makes it out of 'da hood' on their own"

Learning to count on yourself and making good choices gets you into the game. Developing friendships based on mutual respect and understanding gets you to the next level. God gets you the victory! It takes strength to survive 'da hood', so when you do get out, give something back. 'Da hood' will make you what you will become. 'Da hood' will test you, and every time you pass the test you will get stronger. My son, when you make it out, come back and give some of that strength back to the place and people who helped to make you who you are.

My son...

"Save the drama fo' yo' mama'"

Lying and complaining won't do you any good,especially when the person you're lying and complaining to knows you're lying. 'Keep it real'.'Keep it 100'. 'Man up' and tell the truth. Take your licks, don't whine, that's not manly. You can't make someone listen to or believe that drama. Now mama', she might listen. She'll listen to anything. That's why she's mama'; as for me, I don't won't to hear it!

My son...

"Don't start none, won't be none"

Don't go out looking for trouble. If you don't look to 'trip', others won't look to 'trip' on you. Trust me on this.

My son…

"Don't go out like 'Willie Lump Lump'"

"Fool me once, shame on you". "Fool me twice, shame on me". "Fool me three times" just call me 'Willie Lump Lump'. "Who is Willie Lump Lump?" you ask. Willie Lump Lump is the 'fool's, fool'. This guy (or girl) that never learns their lesson. They keep falling for the same trick over and over. My son, don't let anybody 'bump yo' head', fool you, trick you, use you. If they do, don't fool with them anymore. If they say they're sorry, that's cool but don't give them another chance to trick you again. I ain't gonna' lie to you, I've been tricked before. So I've been 'Willie Lump Lump', once. It happens to everybody. The test is not to keep letting it happen. Don't get used, or be a user. I taught you better than that.

My son...

"Word is bond"

Whatever you say, do. Whatever you promise, keep. Your word is your life-line. Don't throw it out unless you really mean it. Your word will save you when nothing else can. Trust me on this.

My son...

If someone is talking to another person and not you, stay out of it. That's how people get hurt (unless its for moral reasons). If a person is having a problem with their girlfriend, stay out of it. The girlfriend will turn on you and help her boyfriend. Trust me on this. Now, other than this one situation, always help a lady out. Always.

My son...

"Don't be like the blind leading the blind"

Don't follow anybody who doesn't know what they want, what they're doing, or how they're going to get what they want. This happens all the time with young guys who join gangs or get into the drug dealing game. Most of them end up in jail or the grave. Some even strung out on the same drugs they were dealing. Don't throw your life, your future away following 'the blind'. As a matter of fact, don't be a follower. Step to your own beat. Followers put their lives in other people hands so they can blame someone else for what happens to them. How weak is that? If you're gonna' follow someone, follow someone who has taken a path to success. Better yet, blaze your own trail to success.

My son…

"Never date your best friend's sister"

If you do, you will probably mess up both relationships. Because each will blame you if something goes wrong. If either of them (your sister or your friend) ask you about the other, just stay out the mix. This is a train wreck waiting to happen. My best friend's sister use to like me when we were young. I use to tell her I liked her too much to messup our friendship by dating her. She thought that I was just making excuses. But when we got older she came to me and said she understood. When you're young, you just go with your emotions. Your emotions will change, your friendship with someone shouldn't. Don't mess up a good thing by giving in to your emotions. Now I have two good friends for the rest of my life. Trust me on this.

My son...

"About the color of your skin..."

The color of your skin doesn't make you who you are. It's your mind, your thoughts, your consciousness, your beliefs, your actions. If by your actions you hurt black people, if by your talk you talk down on black people, if in your mind you hate black people, then you hate yourself. If you hate black people (or any other person just because of their skin color, then that's wrong). It's o.k. to feel good about yourself, yourpeople. Just as long as you are fair with all people and respect all people. "Treat others as you want to be treated." But first you gotta' want to treat yourself well, to love who you are. You can't love others until you learn to love yourself. Remember, it's not theoutside, but the inside that matters.

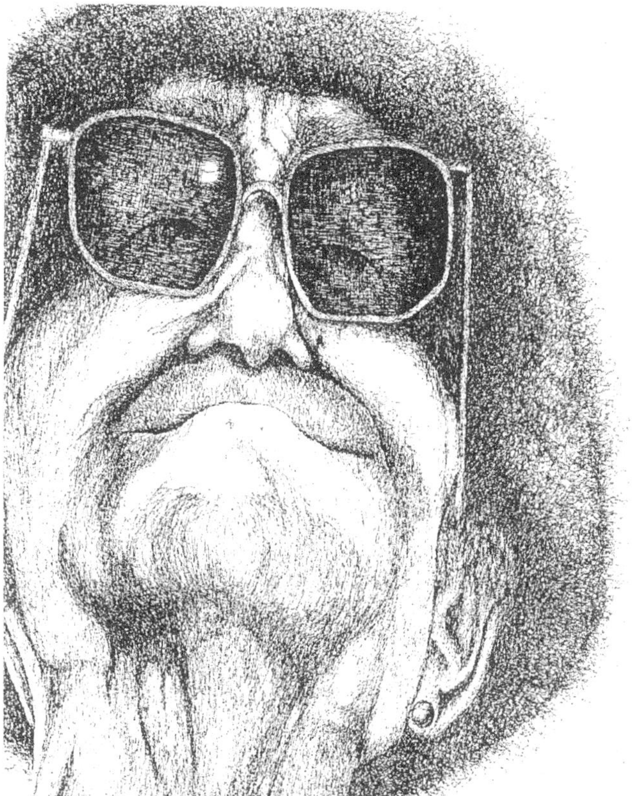

GRAND PEOPLE
By Carolyn Dennis-Roundtree

They lived their lives without worry.

Always giving respect
to the times and deeds of their forefathers.

Now generations later and hundreds of
memories now understood.

I dream about these "Grand People."
Wanting to know how they survived
slavery, share cropping, migrant working
with dignity and respect.
With pieces of their true culture
still intact.
How they managed to live happy
lives and share moments of laughter
in between, no or low pay,
Jim Crowism, hard times, harsh times.

Wish I knew the secrets of these
(major me gustaria saber los secretos)
"Grand People"
(de estas personas grandiosas)
better.

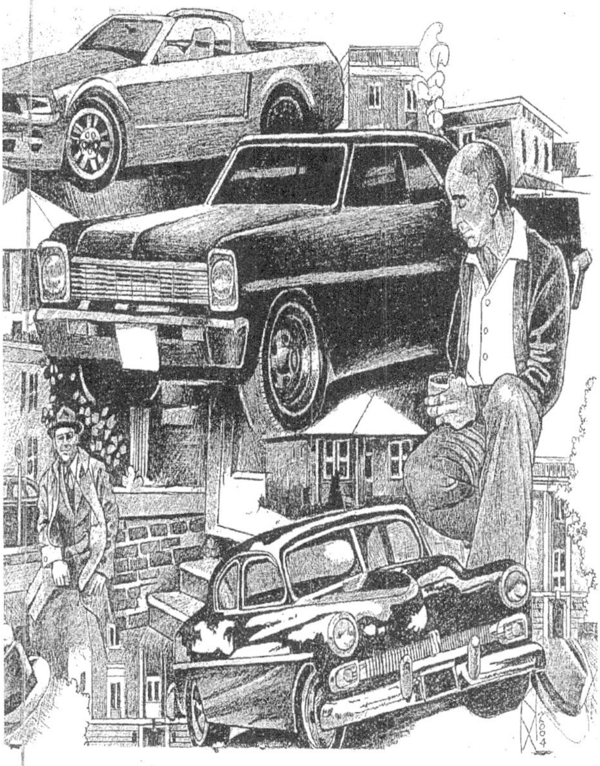

Rites of Passage-Kinship System

What can you and others do to change something that's not right? Explain below.

Part II

"On the Real"

My son...

"Bullets do have a name. Sometimes that name is the innocent"

Unfortunately, in 'da hood' any place at any time, can be the wrong place at the wrong time. Try to stay involved in sports, in church, in family events and youth clubs. No, there's no guarantee that nothing bad will happen, even while you're participating in these activities, at these places, but the chances are less that they will. Anyway, that's what helped me, that and the prayers of my mother. My son, I'm praying for you. In 'da hood', death is always just around the corner and right across the street. So always look both ways.

My son...

"Niggaz are like flies, they're always around some shit"

Some people are always around trouble. These foul people seem to attract trouble like 'flies on shit'. A 'nigga' (I don't care how you spell it) is the person who wants you to be a failure, like them. Being a 'nigga' has nothing to do with their race. People of all races can be 'niggaz'. A 'nigga' is a negative, foul, hateful person. Here's the 'nigga test'. If you are trying to do something positive, something that will get you out of 'da hood' (gangs, drugs, violence), the 'nigga' is the one telling you "You crazy. You ain't going nowhere". My son, stay away from all 'niggaz', and above all, don't be a 'nigga'. There ain't nothing cool about being a 'nigga'. Trust me on this.

Get back with me at michaeldennism@aol.com

My son...

"You could die over a dime
It's the principle that matters"

In 'da hood', if you put a person in the position where they have to check you (yes even for a dime), then they will. And yes, they will hurt you, even for a dime. I ain't lying, I've seen it happen. It's not the dime, it's the principle . The what doesn't matter, it's always about the why. You will be dealt with, you can count on it. Their 'rep' depends on it. Nobody's going to let you punk them for anything, they can't. So are you willing to get hurt for a dime? Then don't trip. It ain't worth it. In 'da hood' there's no such thing as a 'little thing'. Always 'do the right thing' by people whether it seems like a little thing or not. Trust me on this.

My son...

> "Gangs are like extended families, except, they're dysfunctional"

A lot of gangs tell you, "You gotta get 'beat down' in order to 'be down'. My son, don't join anything that requires you to be 'beat down' or 'broken' down in order to 'be down'. They only show you love so they can control you. If something was to happen to you, their 'so called' love won't do you any good. Real family, functional families give 'unconditional' love. There's nothing you can do, or have to do to earn it. It's yours just because you're family.

My son...when you grow up,

"Your manhood, your money, your woman, you never give up. In that order"

This is half true... If someone pulls a gun on you, let them have your money. They got the best hand for now. You can make some more money, but not if you're dead. If your girlfriend wants to leave you, let her go. Don't ever try to make someone stay with you if they don't want to. Now, if someone disrespects your 'manhood', (doesn't respect you as a man) well, that's different. Then it's an 'eye for an eye'. You're gonna' have to stand up for yourself. I'm not talking about using violence, violence should be used only for self-defense, if at all. My son, you gotta' speak up for your manhood, that's all you got. On the other hand never test another man's manhood. This test you can't win. Trust me.

My son...

"Unfortunately, in 'da hood' people die all the time. Most for nothing"

(Be it by drive by shootings, drug overdose, AIDS, suicide etc.). I know this isn't cool, and doesn't make any sense, but it's real. I feel sorry that this is happens. That's why I'm trying to save your life. Your life is the one life that matters to me right now. If I can save you my son, you can save your son's life, and he can save his son's life. If I have to die so that you can live, I will. At least I won't die for nothing, like so many in 'da hood' do. These life lessons are the greatest gift a father can pass down to his son. Always remember that.

My son...

"If you get caught up in the game, there's a jail cell or a bullet with your name"

Sometimes bullets do have names. Every time you feed into that drama out there, you make yourself a target. By this, I mean getting involved with gangs, selling drugs, disrespecting the police, lying and stealing. These things can have deadly consequences. You can die for wearing the wrong colors. When it comes down to drug game, there's no such thing as 'homies'. It's every man for themselves. They ain't playing. If they can't get to you, they might go after yo' family. The best thing to do is to steer clear of all that drama. On the real, if you get caught up in the game, you can bet there is a jail cell or a bullet with your name. Trust me on this.

My son...
   "Any coward can pull a trigger
   or hit a girl"

Neither of these will make you a man. Matter of fact, it will make you a coward. How shameful. These are the easy ways out of dealing with your problems. It doesn't make you 'hard', it makes you soft. It takes more out of you than it puts in you. Once done, it can't be undone and it won't make you a man. As a matter of fact, it takes a man to not pull a trigger. It takes a man to keep his hands off a girl (there is never a good reason to hit a lady). A real man finds other ways to deal with his problems. Pulling a trigger or hitting a girl ain't it. Trust me on this.

My son...

"In 'da hood' sometimes the innocent gets hurt, but almost always the ignorant gets killed"

I ain't gonna' lie to you, on occasion, the innocent find themselves in the 'wrong place at the wrong time'. Sometimes they get hurt, or God forbid, killed. But most times they survive. On the other hand, the ignorant, through their stupidity, keeps putting themselves in the path of danger. To be honest, most times nothing happens to them, but that makes them do more and more stupid stuff until they get hurt, or God forbid, killed. My son, don't be stupid. All young people think it won't happen to them, until it does. Sooner or later your number is going to come up. But I guarantee you this, the more stupid choices you make, the sooner your number will come up. Trust me on this.

My son…

"In 'da hood', it's everyman for himself"

Don't be foolish enough to think that there's somebody in those streets that 'really' cares about you. Watch. When something jumps off, who do they look out for? I'll tell you who, themselves, as they should. You better do the same. Son, whatever it takes, always look out for number one. You.

My son….

> "If you gotta' run to get a gun, 'respect' you gets none"

This is weak! You have allowed your false sense of who you are (pride) to take over your ability to make good choices. So what, you may be a little embarrassed because somebody 'dissed' you. You gonna get a gun for that, for real? You gotta' be kidding! Whoever 'dissed' you will get their turn to get 'dissed' (remember you reap what you sew). Trust me on this, let that 'lightweight' stuff go. Lil punks run and get a gun every time something happens to them. You're better than that.

My son...

"Violence isn't the way"

Try to avoid violence at all cost. I don't like it, I wish it wasn't happening, but I take it serious and so should you. Don't be afraid of the violence, but don't run to it either. When it goes down, go the other way. Let someone tell you about it later (if you're interested, and I hope you aren't). This is why innocent people get hurt (this is when you should 'mine your own'). My son, don't be drawn to violence, seek out peace.

Get back at me michaeldennism@aol.com

My son...

"Survival is 'by any means necessary"

Seek out all available avenues for your survival, study all possible consequences for your actions, and always choose with caution. Sometimes what may look like a good choice may be a bad choice in disguise.

Get back at me <u>michaeldennism@aol.com</u>

My son...

> "The streets are like battle grounds; 'killing fields'"

Some are born to it, some choose, others are chosen. Here survival is 'day-to-day'. Those who have no future make their homes here. It's the 'call of the wild'. It's the 'Kiss of Death'. For awhile it seems cool...until the bodies start to fall. But by then it's too late, because when 'you're in, you're in'. "Blood in, blood out'. 'One way in, and one way out', and that's death. My son, this isn't for you. You have so much more to offer. Don't listen to that 'call of the wild'. As you get older, its voice will become less and less audible. Trust me on this.

Baby I'm for Real
Dreaming Casually
J. MORALES
H84427 P.O. Box 290066
REPRESA, CA. 95671-0066

My son...

"You gotta' bring some, to get some"

I don't like it, but I understand it. In 'da hood', you gotta' let them know that you ain't no 'easy win'. Let them know that they gotta' 'bring some to get some'. They need to know that if they are going to step to you, then you are going to step back to them. They need to know that they can lose just as much as they're trying to take from you. That's the only way they're going to understand that it ain't worth trippin' about. We call that 'bring some to get some'. Once they know you're willing to go 'toe-to-toe', they'll leave you alone. Trust me on this.

My son...

"Everybody don't make it out (or want to make it out) 'da hood'"

Some aren't strong enough, some aren't tough enough, some aren't smart enough, some don't want to leave, some can't leave. There are different ways to make it out of 'da hood' (there's physically, there's mentally, there's spiritually), or all three. 'Da hood' isn't all negative i.e., gangs, drugs, violence etc. There are a lot of good people in 'da hood' who do good things every day. Being in the 'da hood' doesn't bother them, they love it. There's a lot of good in 'da hood', a lot of fun, a lot of family and friends. For these 'cool' people, they have risen above the 'negativity'. My son, rise above the negativity of 'da hood', no matter where you end up living.

My son...

"Threats are to be taken seriously"

I ain't gonna' lie to you, if someone threatens you, believe them and take the appropriate action. The rule is to 'not give the person threatening you a chance to carry out their threat'. This doesn't means to get them before they get you. It means to dosomething about it. Let somebody know, so that if you have to protect yourself (self-defense) somebody knows why. When you let someone know, most times things get worked out before they get crazy. Most threats start small and get bigger, that's why it's better to deal with them sooner rather than later. My son, don't ever make treats, but certainly take <u>all</u> treats seriously. On the real, your life should be just as important to you, as theirs is to them. I've been there. I know what I'm talking about.

My son…

"Sometimes you get a 'ass whippin'"
"Sometimes you give a 'ass whippin'"

Either way, don't trip. If you get beat up, don't trip, let it go. If the person wants to fight again, then fight, just don't start the fight. Sooner, rather than later, you're going to win. If you win the fight, don't trip, let it go. Don't brag or boast, or try to embarrass the person you fought. This will earn you respect and street 'cred'. Not because of the fight, but because you showed some class after the fight. Even if they don't like you, they will respect you. Later in life, that same person may end up being one of your best friends. Trust me on this.

Get back at me michaeldennism@aol.com

My son...

The big question, "When should you have sex?" The answer, I can't tell you. It depends on how mature you are. I didn't say it depends on if you want to, (of course you will want to). I said it depends on your maturity. Maturity means, can you handle the consequences, the responsibility of being sexually active? Are you ready to take care of a baby if need be? Are you able to help the mother and baby out financially? Are you ready to deal with catching a Sexually Transmitted Disease? Are you willing to die for sex? If you're hardheaded like I was, you're probably gonna do what you want, not what you should. So protect yourself (use a condom). I don't care what she says, use a condom. I don't care how good it feels, use a condom. Don't get caught in that baby trap. One night of pleasure can lead to a lifetime of pain. But if you do make a baby, then take care of your baby. That's real talk.

STRONGER THAN THE STREETS
(fuerte como las calles)
By Michael Dennis

I've only seen it a few times
but I've seen it enough to know it's real.
A love that's stronger than the streets,
stronger than the street code "kill or be killed."

This love I speak comes in these forms.
The first is the love of a "good" girlfriend.
A girlfriend that sees beyond the neighborhood.
A girlfriend that brings you out,
instead of keeping you in.
She's the one who says, "I'm not like that."
Her actions, her spirit tells you she's true,
and that to stay with her, you need to be better.
Respect her in what you say, and what you do.

And as a reward, you begin to see things clearer.
The shadow of death fades
and the light comes nearer.

Of course your "so called" homies begin to hate.
All haters hate when you have
something they want.
But your true homies will be happy for you,
no doubt.
And the haters will end up where haters go;

"The Joint."

A love that's stronger than the street

The second love I've seen is the love of mom.
Moms who still showed you love through
 your "hard head" days.
When you knew everything,
didn't want to do anything.
And broke her heart,
sent her to her knees to pray.
Your moms; who went to school
when you acted a fool.
Your moms; who went to court,
when you broke the legal rules.
Your moms; who refused to be embarrassed
that you were her child.
And every time you "tripped", she caught you,
when you were completely wild.

Your moms; when the bullets were flying
and your "homies" ducked for cover.
She said, "Kill me, but spare my baby."
that's why 'til death, you love her.

That's why you have the *courage* to say,
"Enough is enough."
Your mother's love is
than any street stuff.
And don't let me forget the love of your dad.

Who says, "If you hurt him, you hurt me."
"My life for his life. He's all that I have."
"And the only 'hood he's claiming
is my house, my 'hood."
No "street codes" can stand against
 this kind of manhood.

A love that's stronger than the streets

And the last, but certainly not least,
is the love of God.
I've seen new programs that promise this,
promised that...
But soon they all were "kicked to the curb",
 and died.
Money wasted, young lives wasted,
check out the facts.
The fact that these are real young lives, not toys.

These are breathing and thinking young girls
 and boys.
"Just Say No", doesn't work, nor does
 "Believe You Can Fly."
Because in their real world its "I think I could die.
So I must "Do or Die."
"Don't talk about it, "Be" about it."
So all that man has tried to do for them
has failed them. No, none can say, "I succeed".
Until they were shown the love of God.
And to receive this great gift,
 all they did was believe.

I've seen hard core killer kids break
  down and cry.
I've seen street dealers, give up everything,
and go completely dry.
I've seen run-a-ways, lost strays,
give up their street ways.
Not for a minute, but for the rest of their days.
I've seen young girls, who grew up in a rush.
Back up, get their respect,
get back their parent's trust.
I've seen children that hated their parent's guts...
Break down and cry saying, "Mom, I'm sorry.
I love you so much."
I've seen failing students,
become honor students overnight.
I've seen the young "walking dead"
  choose the light.

I've seen young hard-core gang members say,
"I'm claiming the Lord."
And because of the love they had for him,
so did his homeboys.
I've seen young street leaders
  become street preachers.

I've seen a "Most Wanted"
*enemy, be given a pass,
because he chose God over the 'hood.
Don't front, don't laugh.
I've seen someone pull a gun
to kill a young hood'...

But God spared him, not for evil, but for His good.
I've seen a Crip and a Blood,
 show each other love.

I've seen Brown and Black, get each other's back.

I've seen hate, turn to like, turn to love,
all because they chose the love
of the God from above.

The loves that are stronger than the streets...
Are the loves that play for keeps.

That's how we can change their world, and ours.

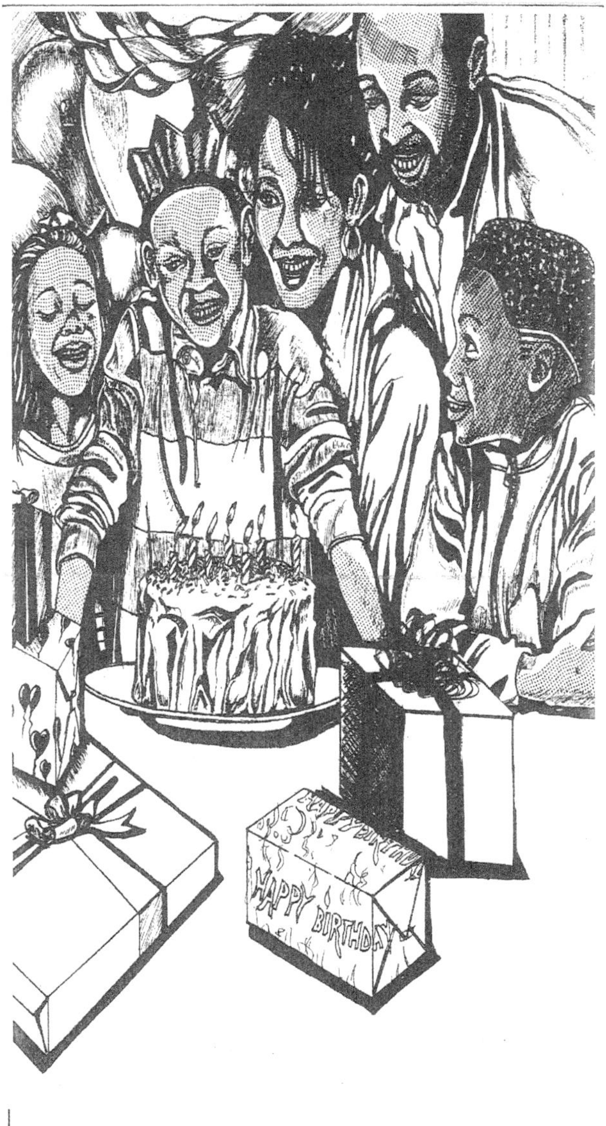
HAPPY BIRTHDAY

Rites of Passage- Overcoming Negative Environments

The poem mentions four loves that are stronger than the streets (girlfriend, mother, father, and God)

Which one (or more) of these "loves" within your own life do you feel can help to overcome negative environments? Explain below.

Part III

"Back in the Day"

Affirmation (Afirmacion)
    by Carolyn Dennis-Roundtree

I believe in dreams, peace, being rich,
being better.
In becoming one with

the God force.
I believe in family.
In the visions of us... young ones.
I believe that each generation must
help the next.

I believe in the positive force
of friendship based on trust and
common values.
I believe in revolution.
One must take place
if we are to break the mental chains
that keeps us from soaring, uniting.
From becoming a better people,
a greater nation.

I believe in positive changes.
I believe in the ancestors
who continue to cover our
lives with seeds of hope.

And I believe in *(y yo creo en)*
Me *(mi)*…
in us.

Because…
We are young
gifted
beautiful
and that's a fact.

We are the future.

My son...

> "Grandma' and Grandpa'
> gets much respect"

From birth to death, I've taught this to you. If you disrespect your mother's mother, your life will be very hard. But if you show respect to your mother and her mother (grandma') you will have a good life. Trust me on this.

My son...

> A praying mother's prayers
> are always answered.

Thank God for that. What do you think has saved you from some of the dumb things you've done so far...your mother's prayers. What do you think it was that stopped you from doing some of the things you wanted to do but didn't, or from going to some of the places you wanted to go to, but shouldn't have...your mothers prayers. All those times you fell, and got back up was because of your mother's (and grandmother's) prayers. How do I know, because it was my mother's prayers that got me through as well.

My son...

"Your house is to be protected from being disrespected"

Where you live is a 'special' place. Be you a man, young man, or boy. If you are a man, never let anybody disrespect your house. If you are a young man or boy, don't bring disrespect to your parents' house by letting your friends bring over girls, drugs, alcohol etc., and tell you what to do in your parents' home. How weak is that? This is about personal power and pride. Give these up and you have nothing. Trust me on this.

My son...

"Back in the day"

Children were asked to leave the room when the conversation or activities turned to what we call 'grown folk' stuff. I know some of your friends' parents are allowing you guys to stay in the room during some of these 'grown folk' conversations and activities, but that's not cool. So when adults start doing 'grown folk stuff', leave the room. Trust me, you have the rest of your life to grow up. But right now, you should be allowed to enjoy being a kid. Later you're going to have plenty of time to be 'grown'. And when this happens, you're going to wish you were a kid again. Trust me on this.

My son...

    'Back in the Day'
"Children were seen, not heard"

In the company of adults, keep a low profile. Use these moments to see how adults interact with each other. Learn what to do and what not to do. This doesn't mean that you don't matter, it means that there's a time and place for all things. Be patient, my son, your time is coming. Sooner than you think, trust me on this one.

SPIRITS WAITING (espiritus esperando)
   By Carolyn Dennis-Roundtree

Tired of seeing,
hearing about young black men
young brown men
African men, Mexican men, Chicano men
Native American men
European men and women
being suicidal (from too much pressure)
genocidal (from too much hate)
homicidal (from too much "self-hatred")
Victims of mind games

and historical
ignorance.

Forgetting those seeds
of victory
planted by Nat Turner (free your body)
Queen Nefertiti
Emperor Hallie Salasie
Confucious, Emiliano Zapata
Harriet Tubman, Fredrick Douglass
Angela Davis
"Chief Sitting Bull" (free you spirit)
Cesar Chavez
Malcolm X, Maya Angelou
Elijah Mohammed

Francisco (Pancho) Villa
Pocahontas, Geronimo
Madame CJ Walker
Marcus Mosiah Garvey
Hillary Clinton
Dr. Martin Luther King Jr. ("Free at Last")
Nelson Mandela
John and Robert Kennedy
William (Bill) Jefferson Clinton
Barack and Michelle Obama
Mother Teresa
Roberto Duran
Rosa Parks
Ghandi
Oprah Winfrey
PD ("Puff Daddy"), Kanye West...
These "Freedom Fighters..."
Whose Seeds
know not color,
only character.
(simillas cual color no saben solo caracter)

Lay, sleeping
in your spirit...
waiting...

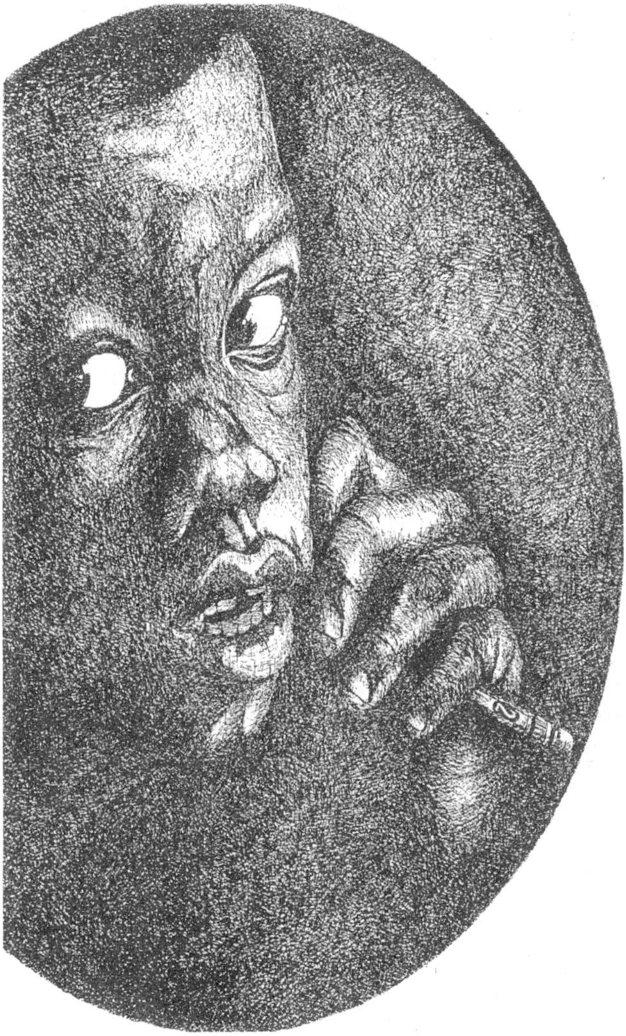

"Hoop Dreams" (True Story) "Ride or Die?"

Young Michael has been living in the same neighborhood for the past ten years. He and his brothers and close friends from the neighborhood are very close. They play sports together and have come to each other's aid many times. Because of the neighborhood they live in, Michael has been exposed to gangs, drugs and alcohol, crime and violence for most of his young life. Some of his friends/associates and other family members are involved in gangs (including his brothers but not his close friends) but Michael, although exposed, doesn't claim. Michael loves sports (and is pretty good at it too) and one day wishes to become a "professional" basketball player (a promise he made to himself). One day Michael is told that two of his brothers (the two which are gang related) has been shot, but not killed, by so called rival gang members. Michael also learns that earlier, his two brothers had shot and wounded members of this rival

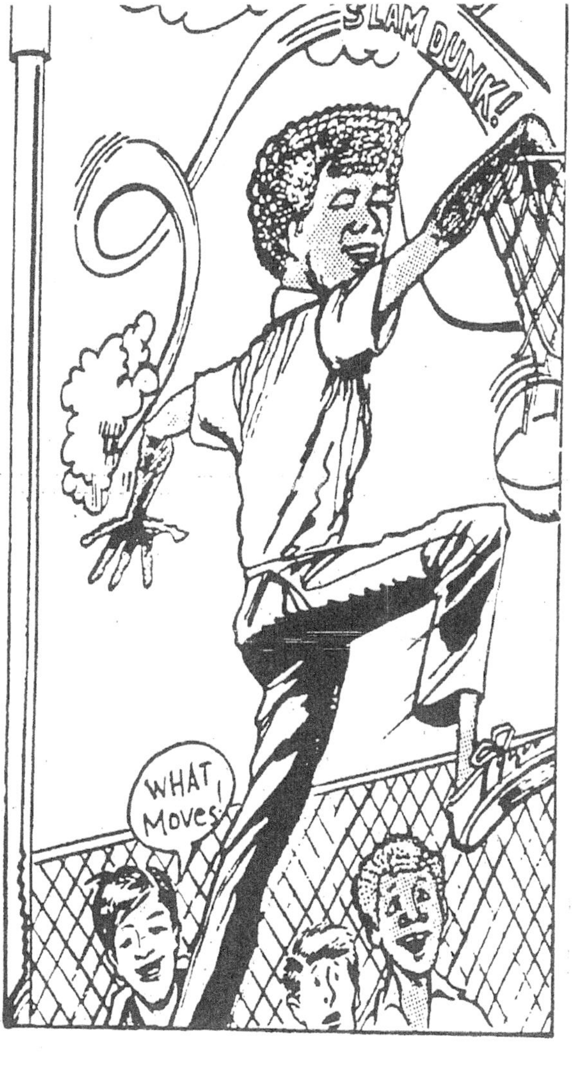
SLAM DUNK!
WHAT MOVES!

gang. Michael is furious, frustrated and confused. On the one hand, he feels he must retaliate for his brothers. He can't let anybody get away with that. That's disrespecting his family. On the other hand, he is aware of what his brothers did earlier. That night some of his brothers' "homies" came by and asked him to "go and ride on them fools who shot his brothers". "Ride or Die." What would you do?

Michael chose not to go. Since his brothers were still alive he didn't trip. But he did find out what the problem was and spoke to the brothers of the other guys to squash it. So Michael went on to college (a primarily "white" university) where he met good people of all races, cultures and ethnicities (people he still consider as friends to this very day). He played ball, received his college degree and had a great time. He didn't go "pro" in basketball, but he did go "pro" another way (just as he promised himself).
He became a successful public school

teacher who is committed to giving back something positive to where he came from. He's teaching the lesson of "One world, One people, One race, One love." Instead of "Ride or Die", he chose to "Lead and Succeed." He chose to "Live and let Live" instead of "Kill or be Killed."

Rites of Passage: Appreciation of Life cycle

a. "My Future Goals"

b. What I Need To Do To Achieve My Goals

c. "Why I Will Succeed"

d. "How Long It Will Take"

UMOJA
By Carolyn Dennis-Roundtree

We strive to be community,
brothers and sisters.
Look out for each other.

But we remain divided
by the "other world's" definitions,
and the false god of material things.
It all keeps out the Umoja spirit.
The rebirth from within.
Umoja is unity with country, with society,

with community, family
and friends.
Is the first day of Kwanzaa.
Is a celebration of
what must be.

Umoja spirit
within,
without it
nothing is possible.

Let us unite.
All people,
all colors...
one race.

The human race.

In love *(en amor).*
In peace *(en paz).*
Forever *(para siempre).*

Rites of Passage – Respect for Traditions and Heritage . Do you believe we should respect each others 'traditions and heritage and...

> "...unite all people...all colors....one race, the human race, in love, in peace forever."

Explain why/why not below.

What will you personally do to respect other peoples and their cultures. Explain below.

HOME GROWN VARIETY
(variedad crecida en casa)
By Carolyn Dennis-Roundtree

A seed
from the original continent
flowers

here.

A transplant among garden variety
types.

A mixture of Black, Brown, White,
and others.
That has only a faint sense
of their original source.

The soil that grew the "real"
flowers that <u>blow</u> a fragrance
that smells like freedom.

I wonder can this "new breed"
of young Black, Brown, White, and others
be taught to dance to the old songs
of Africa, of Central America, of Europe,
of Asia, of Latin America,
of the "Middle East"

**here
in the "West"
in America
together?**

In the rhythm of brotherly love...

I hope, yes.
(yo espero que si)

Rites of Passage– Respect for Traditions and Heritage

Do you respect your freedom? Explain why or why not.

Do you respect those who fought for and won the freedoms that you now enjoy? Tell why and how, or why not.

My son....

The end of the matter...
"God moves in mysterious ways"

You are more than a survivor. You are a conqueror. You are conquering the debilitating effects of crime, drugs, violence and poverty that you are exposed to growing up in 'da hood'. No wonder you're so tough. You're young, but you're strong. And you're going to be a heck of a man. My man, go on with yo' baaaad self!

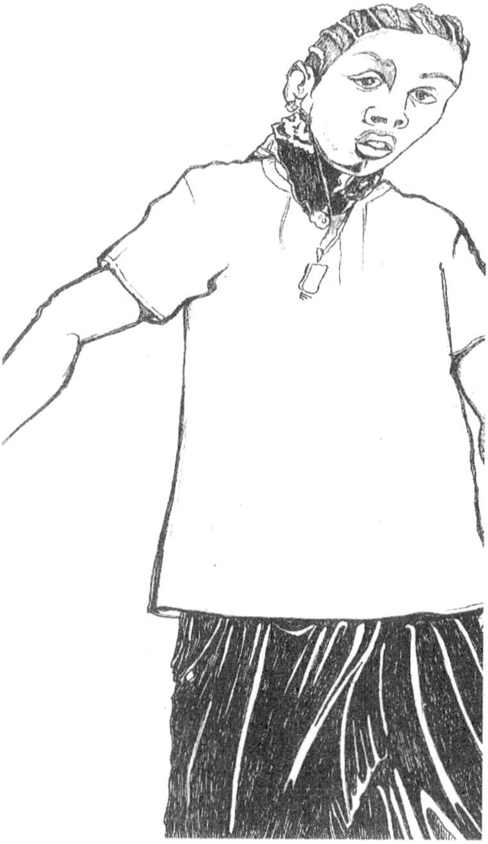

Made in the USA
Monee, IL
15 June 2020